Stray Moments

Poems
by
Joyce Meyers

BLUE LIGHT PRESS ✦ 1ST WORLD PUBLISHING

SAN FRANCISCO ✦ FAIRFIELD ✦ DELHI

Winner, 2024 Blue Light Poetry Prize

Stray Moments

Copyright ©2025 by Joyce Meyers

All rights reserved. Printed in the United States of America. No part of this book may be used or reproduced in any manner whatsoever without written permission except in the case of brief quotations embodied in critical articles and reviews. For information contact:

1st World Library
PO Box 2211
Fairfield, IA 52556
www.1stworldpublishing.com

Blue Light Press
www.bluelightpress.com
bluelightpress@aol.com

Book & Cover Design
Melanie Gendron
melaniegendron999@gmail.com

Cover Photo
free art from pexels.com

Author Photo
David Phillips

First Edition

Library of Congress Cataloging-in-Publication Data

ISBN: 978-1-4218-3575-4

Acknowledgments

"To you, listening," *Philadelphia Poets*, Spring 2015

"At Great Falls," *Paterson Literary Review*, Spring, 2023

"Rescue," *Common Ground Review*, Spring/Summer 2019

"Redtail," *Atlanta Review*, Fall/Winter 2024

"The joy of grapefruit on a rainy morning," *Evening Street Review*, Summer 2023

"Why I always cry at weddings," *Adanna Literary Journal*, Fall, 2022

"Seasons," *Iodine Poetry Journal*, Fall/Winter 2013/2014

"Patience," *Ibbetson Street*, Fall, 2011

"Overtones," *Loch Raven Review*, November 2024

"October morning," *Humana Obscura*, Fall/Winter 2023

"Snow," *Schuylkill Valley Journal*, Spring 2015

"December light," *The Comstock Review*, Winter, 2024/2025

"Early Robins," *Across the Long Bridge*, Dec. 2005 (Lulu Books)

"Refulgence," *Humana Obscura*, 2023

"In the Borghese Gardens," *Philadelphia Poets*, Spring 2007

"Dream Thief," *Philadelphia Poets*, Spring 2007

"Inukshuk," *White Pelican Review*, Spring 2008

Contents

To you, listening 1
At Great Falls 2
Morning at the beach 3
Rescue 4
Undertow 5
Redtail 6
Feathers, strewn 7
Eating an ice cream cone: a gender thing 8
The joy of grapefruit on a rainy morning 10
Why I always cry at weddings 11
Intimations 12
Seasons 13
Patience 14
Overtones 15
On the cusp 16
Autumn Equinox 18
Autumn chords 19
Bend in the creek 20
October morning 21
Snow 22
December light 23
Early Robins 24
Refulgence 25
How evening falls 26
In the Borghese Gardens 27
Dream Thief 28
Phra Sowanak 29
Inukshuk 30
About the Author 33

To you, listening

Do not let my silver hair deceive you.

I am a hatchling. Face smeared
with yolk. Wet wings. Voice
as cracked as the shell
that lately was my home.

I long to fly, to sing,
to tell you something true.

Curved white neck of a swan
        gliding across yellow leaves
                reflected in blue water.

In another life I was a girl running
on a beach. Arms wide, hair
catching the wind. Even now
the taste of salt air fills me.
The taste of tears.

I want to feed you from a ceramic bowl
hand-painted by a dark-eyed girl
with slender fingers
on the southern coast of Italy.
Pattern of lemons, purple
grapes, vine tendrils.

        Sweet juice mingling
                with tartness on your tongue.
                    Be nourished.

Say: *Yes, I see.*

At Great Falls

The boulders lay where the earth
tossed them, weightless, for an instant,
as grains of rice tossed at a wedding,
then immobile for eons
while water found a way
around, between. Pewter shapes

the wind and water made
say nothing of the unseen hand
that tossed them there
to delight my sight. Watching
from the shore, I am as they,
brought here from somewhere far
at random, as ions spun,

collided into cells.
So many moments shaped
this moment, some illusioned
by a sense of choice, as if each step
did not, does not, follow
from what has gone before,
the convoluted path a double helix
of a history only dimly felt.

Under the sun they glisten,
bask in solid repose while all around
is movement. Downstream,
past falling cascades crashing
over cliffs, the surface smooths,
fish flash silver, ripple the water.

A great blue heron stretches its neck,
imitating sculpture.

Morning at the beach

Flocks of sandpipers
chase ebbing tides
then flee the incoming waves,
their upside-down doubles
mirrored on wet sand.

As beach walkers approach
a hundred birds move as one,
circling as the sun glints
off white underbellies, a swirl
of silver confetti against blue sky.

I walk for miles
past the broken pier
sentried by silhouetted gulls
trying to read the signs.

What morning brings
the tides take back.
The sun shines no less
brightly for being mortal.

Rescue

Two nights ago the tide vomited
jellyfish; thousands dotted the beach
for miles. In the morning no one swam
or walked along the shore,
though curious children poked
at the translucent blobs.

My grandson found a space
to build a sandcastle, dug
a wide moat, and pronounced it
a jellyfish preserve.
With his shovel he collected
as many as he could,
dropped them in,
never asking if they
were still alive.

This morning's beach is clean,
scoured by the moon's bright hands.
No jellyfish, no sandcastles.
My grandson is philosophical,
believes the waves that razed his castle
helped the jellyfish he saved
to swim back home. Today
he builds a spaceship in the sand.

Undertow

Low tide, mosaic of broken shells. Children
       dig for crabs, build drip castles in wet sand.

All will be gone by morning. The tide creeps
       in like a lazy snake, wets the shore, recedes.

Speckled sandpipers on toothpick legs
       chase ebbing surf, pull wriggling creatures

from the mud, flee the incoming wave.
       Eat and run, rude dance of survival.

Mothers calling to children suck in their stomachs,
       forget how stretch marks give them away.

Don't go out too far! Watch out for the undertow!
       Beyond the breakers a calm surface

catches the sun. Somewhere between
       here and the horizon sharks circle,

whales breach, dive deep,
       mouths open for krill.

Redtail

The first surprise that he was there
at all. We had glimpsed them in treetops,
perched on wires above the roads,
circling among clouds, watching
for any movement on the ground
that might be breakfast. Never before
this close, just yards from our front door,
next to the Chinese cherry so lately leafless.
The second surprise his size, so hard
to comprehend from a distance. Yet nothing
majestic here. This is a reality show,
earthy as excretion. Whatever
that creature was, it's now a meal,
pulled apart with such total absorption
that my approach, camera and binoculars
in hand, hardly registers. I squint to identify
the long thing dangling from his mouth,
wonder aloud if it's a rodent's tail.
You think it's an intestine. We watch, riveted,
this transubstantiation from dead flesh
to sinew, beak, and wing.

Feathers, strewn

The morning air drips peace
along the lake. I drink it in.
No sound but bird song
and the swish of leaves
streaking cobalt water
with dappled shades of green.

A gray feather on the trail
catches my eye. It's big,
could only be an eagle's.
I admire its sleekness,
its softness, its subtle shades
of gray. Soon I spot another
in the brush, then more
scattered widely along the trail
and in the wood beyond,

testament to something
more than mere molting.
Clearly, there was high drama
here. Yet, how? How did
a predator become prey,
a raptor, snatched?

No witness to this moment,
no one to mourn or tell the tale,
nothing left of breath,
sinew, power, the majesty of flight
but a peaceful morning marked
by a mass of feathers, strewn.

Eating an ice cream cone: a gender thing

Summer solstice, and the sweet air
of evening cries out for ice cream,
the true way to say that summer's here.

For her one scoop of mint chocolate chip;
he wants two scoops of death by chocolate.
Her tongue slowly circles the pale green

mound, allows each chocolate chip
to melt before she takes another lick.
They walk and talk as the sun

begins to sink. In half a block
his ice cream's gone, even the cone
only a memory. She stops licking

long enough to notice, tell him
*You don't know how to eat
an ice cream cone! You're*

supposed to lick it slowly.
They stroll for several blocks,
debating the merits of licking

versus biting. He proclaims
the sensual joy of mouthfuls
of smooth cold chocolate

sliding down his throat;
she argues the pleasure
should be savored bit by bit,

the flavor lingering long
while her languorous tongue
works its way around

the shrinking mound. In twenty
minutes, her ice cream done,
they smile, agree to disagree.

I guess it's a gender thing, she says.

The joy of grapefruit on a rainy morning

Sky pearl-gray without the sheen, the ping
of rain lashing the windowpane, I stand
before my sink sectioning a grapefruit.
I am going nowhere, no reason to rush.
I push the serrated knife edge
along each membrane, leaving sections
to float free. Ceiling light glistens
on the droplets of juice, releasing
a hint of citrus scent perfuming
the kitchen air. The knife glides,
responding to my touch like a lover,
as my tongue grows wet with anticipation.
This luscious flesh the perfect shade
of pink is sweet enough with just enough
sour to pucker my lips into a kiss.

Why I always cry at weddings

though I barely know or never met
the happy couple, and the bride
and groom, and all the parents
are dry-eyed. It isn't that I've known

the promise of rosebuds, the heady scent
of blooms, have battled aphids and blackspot,
seen the petals brown, then drop.
It's that despite the odds

that love will slowly fade
to dust, or worse, when I see
the rings slip onto those young fingers
a cactus flower opens in my heart,

compels from hidden wells of hope
my reservoir of rain.

Intimations

The lake a mirror, the woods
on the far shore doubled
and shimmering, the lines
between foliage and sky,
foliage and water blurred.

I squint the image
into streaks of light and color,
see Monet's water lilies
splashed across a museum wall,
sprouting rose and alabaster
in the pond at Giverny
where we held hands
on the Japanese bridge.

In the distance a dot
that could be a duck.

Closer in, clouds drift on the surface
of the water, parallel wisps
pushed by a breeze to shift, connect,
form an angle, showing
how parallel lines *can* meet,
a space between
mathematics and magic.

Such moments that pass
before words can form
to describe them, a futile effort
to catch and keep what can't be kept,
are all I know, maybe all
I ever need, of eternity.

Seasons

Tethered, she waits.
Waits for someone
to dress her, bring
a meal she cannot taste.
Waits for someone
to turn on the screen
of moving shapes.
Her husband comes
each day, sometimes
her daughter, her son.
I'm a lucky woman, she says.
In spring and summer
they wheel her outside
to sit in the shade.
When the seasons change
she looks through the window,
watches leaves fall,
waits for snow.

Patience

It took just one good rain
to strip the Japanese maple.
Yesterday's bouquet
of autumn crimson, today
a red lace circle on the grass,
tomorrow sere brown litter
to be raked, piled,
carted away like trash.
Months of cold dark mornings
before it leafs again.

In the oak's bare high branches
an unmistakable silhouette:
motionless body, swiveling head,
intent on the business
of staying alive. Everything
depends on knowing
when to sit still, when
to swoop down for the kill.

My mother gave up
on life years before
her heart gave out. She lost
her hearing, her memory, her will
to get out of bed, waited
like an obedient child
for permission
to leave the room.

The apple blossom knows
the hour to open, the acorn
knows when to fall.

Overtones

Five years since you last drew
breath and you haven't left me
yet. The timbre
of your voice lingers
in my ear, your soft brown eyes
smile across the breakfast table.
And, yes, I still slip into present
tenses at odd moments
when I least expect it.

On a busy morning
a quick trip to the grocery store
is suddenly transformed
when the car radio plays
Mozart's Clarinet Concerto,
and decades slip away:
to the first time I heard it
in an Atlanta music store
and had to bring it home
to share with you.

It became part of our language,
a way of making love.
I had the Adagio played
at your memorial service,
tears streaming down my face
with the knowledge that you
would never hear it again.

And yet, you're here beside me
in a car you've never seen
while the solo clarinet
sings that plaintive melody
and you touch me
across the void.

On the cusp

Spring equinox again
when day equals night,
dark equals light
and everything hangs
in the balance. Star
magnolias bloom
fragrant white while
just over the horizon
looms a new cold war.
Bluebirds start to nest
while autocrats
tighten their grip around
the throat of democracy,
and we read that we have
seven years to save
the planet before
it's doomed.

The question hangs.

And yet along the creek
sunlight dances
on wet rocks, summons
glints of silver, hints
of green. What are we
to make of this stubborn
earth that showers us
with gifts no matter
what we do while we,
like an abusive spouse,
return its love
with even more abuse?

I teeter on the cusp
of joy and despair,
unable to unsee the rising
seas, the species gone,
the skies abloom
with the brilliance
of spring's abundance.

Autumn Equinox

A blue jay streaks across the yard,
the morning sun on its back.
Brown carpet of newly fallen leaves
still damp from yesterday's downpour.

The gray shroud across the sky
has vanished without a trace.
Against today's deep azure,
green branches tipped with red and gold.

A lone white rose blooms in the side yard.
Crisp oak leaves, windswept,
cling to cherry tomato vines
heavy with deep red globes.

I stand on the cusp
of ripeness and decay,
harvesting tomatoes.
I leave the pale ones on the vine,

knowing an early frost
will kill them. I take the risk
to wait for sweetness.
I hope for a long fall.

Autumn chords

Underfoot, leaves speak
with a raspy voice,
but the creek sings,
rippling over rocks,
while sundrops cavort
through water. Breezes
whisper, kiss skin, argue
with the lesson of leaves.

Dawn's silence, songbirds
already winging south,
syncopates a rhythm
with rush of season's flight.
Summer's serenade lingers
with overtones of echoing
sorrow. Words once
spoken, never to be
unsaid, hang in the air,

rise to a crescendo.
It's all there
in the changing sky,
tones, overtones,
silences, echoes.
How to compose a coda
worthy of it all?

Bend in the creek

At a bend in the creek a boulder
that used to be my heart

glistens silver in the sun.
Once it was a soft pulsing thing

swelling with love until it burst
with grief and scattered

into astral dust. One day
it came to rest in this quiet place

where even dead trees are beautiful
in the late afternoon light –

sculpted roots open to the air
dappled with sun that licks its tongue

into whirls and crevices. Roots, rock
accepting, reflecting whatever washes over.

October morning

Dead leaves flutter in a spider's web
like ghosts of butterflies.

Shimmering reds and golds,
such beautiful dying.

Between seasons
a bit of green lingers,

a lone rosebud
with no time left to bloom.

Along the creek the day
drifts with the current.

Stay with me here
in this place, this time.

Keep winter at bay.

Snow

The snow keeps falling, relentless
as time. There's just no stopping it.
We race to catch it, hold it in our hands.
Moments melt away, ephemeral
as snowflakes, all distinction
lost in the accretion. Shock
of the first gray hair, first
line in the face a mere emblem
of all we can't control.

While the snow falls, we wish
for spring. With each turning
of the earth, what is encrusted
will melt away, what lies
hidden will be revealed. Soft,
vulnerable, ready for worms.

December light

It arrives later, leaves earlier
and while it's here the sun
hangs low as if still leashed to night.
And yet it clamors for attention,
confronting with a radiance
that forces you to turn away.

In these darker days we have no choice
but to view things from a different angle,
to see how the bare bones of trees
hint at the truth of things.

On the chimney next door
a hawk's pale breast glows ruddy
in the morning sun,

and the disappearing days portend
the end of another year, mountains
of tomorrows turning into yesterdays.

The solstice comes and goes
as each day the sun climbs higher,
stays longer, the angle of vision
shifts. Does more daylight
bring less insight?

So little time to see what
winter light reveals.

Early Robins

I saw eight robins yesterday; I slowed
my car to count the ruddy breasts scattered
in the dull green grass, muddy and littered
with trash tossed from cars, mounds of dirty snow.

It's only February, and I know
that spring is long weeks away, it's bitter
cold, and reason says that robins matter
less than politics, war, sports and the Dow.

Though I know they're overused, trite, passé,
as symbol unsophisticated, dead,
guaranteed to make a poem boring,
a child's drawing, the ultimate cliché,

my heart leaped up, as Wordsworth would have said;
I tried to tamp it down, but it kept soaring.

Refulgence

I hear the light singing
before the sun's rim
edges over the ridge.
Pale clouds turn
pinkly resplendent.
This the sparrows know,
start their serenade
even before the stars blink out.
They never read the papers,
rely on other sources
for their news. Unfazed
by darkness, they nest
and breed, visit our feeder
while we sip our coffee,
watch the trees leaf out.

How evening falls

The sun slides down
through branches,
scatters spots of light
across the shadowed yard
onto edges of geraniums
against deep shaded green,
pulls from the petals a hue
more red than any color
seen in sun-splashed day.

So memory wandering
through the gray penumbra
of distant years searches out
the strongest colors –
a sunset painting purple streaks
across pink buttes and cliffs
of the Grand Canyon,
the lambent brown
of your eyes
the first moment
I knew I loved you.

In the Borghese Gardens

I want to remember this:
thick black trunks, curving
branches under dark
canopy, the way some light
slips through, paints patches
of pale yellow-green on shadowed
leaves, highlights a spot of white
on the broad back of a woman.

I want to know her name,
what brings her
to this shaded path
this Tuesday afternoon
and whether someone
loves her.

On the bench
where we stopped to rest
a moment in the shade
I lean my head on your shoulder,
watch her figure fade
into the distance.

Dream Thief

Dawn at the Trevi Fountain,
yesterday's crowd of tourists
still asleep, dreaming
of what they wished for
when their hopeful coins
tinkled on white marble.

No sound now but the rush
of falling water
and the shuffling step
of a man in a yellow shirt,
his trimmed beard
tinged with gray. He's fishing,

not with a hook
but a magnet. He peers
over the fountain's edge,
catches the coins
of greatest value, and slips away
through crooked Roman streets,
his pockets jingling
with other people's dreams.

Phra Sowanak

Chaing Mai, Thailand

Though I met him only once,
I keep his framed picture
on my shelf, a young man
smiling in a saffron robe.

Only nine when his Cambodian mother,
too poor to pay for school,
sent him to the monastery
so he could learn to read.

At twenty-seven he has never
touched a woman.
Never would.
His smile glows like a candle.

He invites us to close our eyes,
breathe slowly and deeply.
Palms upraised, index fingers
touching my thumbs,
I do as he says.

His words rise like lotus blossoms,
unfolding petal by petal.
My heart a caged bird
set free.

Inukshuk*

A pile
of random
rocks beside
a lake or
on a
mountain trail.
A message left by one who passed this way before.
Look closely: It may have a human shape
carefully balanced to resist
the force of wind and rain,
the weight of winter's snow.
Head erect, arms outstretched,
sculpted, engineered,
bearing witness.
Is it an offering to some god,
a warning to a stranger,
a sign of love?
Or only the language
of a human hand reaching
through   time
to say: I   walked
this bit   of earth;
I left   my mark.

*A sculpture formed of rocks, often in a shape suggesting a person, left by anonymous Inuit travelers.

About the Author

Joyce Meyers taught English at the high school and college levels, then embarked on a new career as an attorney, practicing law in Philadelphia for almost three decades. Her poems have appeared in numerous journals and anthologies, including *Atlanta Review*, *The Comstock Review*, *Iodine Poetry Journal*, *Slant*, *Evening Street Review*, *Xanadu*, *Glimpse*, and *Muse Literary Journal*. She won First Prize in the *Atlanta Review* 2014 International Poetry Competition, and has been nominated for a Pushcart Prize. Her published collections include *Twisted Threads* (Kelsay Books, 2024), selected as a Distinguished Favorite by The Independent Press Award; *The Way Back* (Kelsay Books, 2017); and two chapbooks, *Shapes of Love* (Finishing Line Press, 2010), and *Wild Mushrooms* (Plan B Press, 2007).

www.ingramcontent.com/pod-product-compliance
Lightning Source LLC
Chambersburg PA
CBHW031219090426
42736CB00009B/987